"Marketing Strategies That Deliver Amazing Results

How To <u>Sell More</u> <u>By Doing Less</u>"

A practical guide that will help you grasp the importance/benefits of different marketing channels and how to execute them properly.

Richard Roberts

www.**DarkamMarketingServices.com**

www.**videoseowarrior.com**

Blog: www.richardrobertsmarketing.com

Author's Biography

Richard Roberts is the founder of various Internet Marketing solutions including Darkam Marketing Services, Video SEO Warrior, and www.richardrobertsmarketing.com blog.

Richard Roberts founded VideoSEOWarrior.com to promote and provide an easy to follow step-by-step visual approach to assist local businesses owners with the implementation of video marketing strategies to help boost sales and revenue.

I would like to thank you for purchasing my book and I instantly urge you to pay close attention and focus on the information and value you're about to receive. If you're in the process of getting to know how the underlying principles of internet marketing work, this book will open your eyes in terms of the things you really should focus your efforts on and prioritize.

My background in relation to marketing stretches back nearly 15 years. I started out as a door-to-door salesman, selling a cable service in the New York area that was in direct competition with one of the largest cable service provider in the New York area and I then moved on to other marketing ventures. Fast-forward a few years later. I transitioned into the online marketing space and was lucky enough to get in early and see firsthand how my experiences as a salesman would translate online.

Little did I know, the same principles that I had to learn on my own after years of sales experience did actually prove beneficial online, except I felt like I was given a lot more room for error as well as the ability to see near-instant results. The reality of online marketing is that prospects in general don't respond that differently to how they used to years ago, however, the way in which you effectively market and bring value to the forefront is an ever-changing process.

Richard's focus is to simplify internet marketing with tools and techniques that will help local business owners reach more of their ideal customers which will boost revenue profits.

As part of your Kindle Version of this book, I would like to provide you with access to my Video e-course on the benefits of having video commercial for your business.

1. Powerful Statistics On Video Marketing For Small Businesses

2. Custom Video Commercials How It Benefits You

3. Lets Summarize How Video Marketing Can Benefit Your Business

Enjoy,

Marketing Strategies That Deliver Amazing Results

How To Sell More By Doing Less

By Richard Roberts

Table Of Contents

Darkam Marketing Overview

Message From Richard Roberts – CEO Of Darkam Marketing Services

First off, I would like to thank you for downloading my book and I instantly urge you to pay attention and focus in on the information and value you're about to receive. If you're in the process of getting to know how the underlying principles of internet marketing work, this book will open your eyes in terms of the things you really should focus your efforts on and prioritize.

My background in relation to marketing stretches back nearly 15 years. I started out as a door-to-door salesman, selling a cable service in the New York area that was in direct competition with one of the largest cable service provider and I then moved on to other marketing ventures. Fast-forward a few years later. I transitioned into the online marketing space and was lucky enough to get in early and see firsthand how my experiences as a salesman would translate online.

Little did I know, the same principles that I had to learn on my own after years of sales experience did actually prove beneficial online, except I felt like I was given a lot more room for error as well as the ability to see near-instant results. The reality of online marketing is that prospects in general don't respond that differently to how they used to years ago, however, the way in which you effectively market and bring value to the forefront is an ever-changing process.

I've literally spent years of my life reading, studying, and slaving away to learn how efficient marketing strategies are executed, and the results I keep seeing to this day are phenomenal. I read every book that seemed appealing, spent time learning from the most successful marketers firsthand, and every little tweak/tactic you can name in relation to Internet marketing; I've probably done twice.

My experience led me to form a team of people that I know are go-getters by nature and are experts at their respective fields. As a team, we have well over 20 years of individual experience in the online marketing space and all of our team members excel at their respective areas of expertise.

Why You Should Pay Attention

The main reason is because you can literally cut years off your regular learning curve by focusing in on the marketing channels that were proven as effective in different markets for us and hundreds of clients of ours – all of which are foolproof to grasp and their respective benefits you'll find outlined in this guide.

The Darkam Marketing Team/Company Culture

The main thing to emphasize is that we're a very experienced team of marketing consultants who carefully devise efficient strategies for new and established businesses. Our main goal is to ensure our clients see their desired results met while providing the platform for long term, exponential growth.

We have experienced team members who will exclusively focus on certain marketing channels (as part of your overall strategy). Hence, you can trust that the strategies you see on paper will actually be executed with forethought and efficiency. We don't utilize a strategy that works across the board for all clients but rather take our time to create and execute one that is in alignment to your individual company values and goals.

Who Do We Work With?

Our team provides services for established business owners and individuals that are in the process of starting a business or establishing their brand online. We prioritize (and usually choose to work with) businesses whose focus is on providing value for customers over the long run, ones that understand the importance of longevity in business and are prepared to make crucial changes that ensure growth.

Website Development

In the process of considering how to get the most return on every dollar you put into your business, plenty of options open up, but making the right choice is still a serious responsibility, especially if you're looking to expand. We are basically a company that has conducted massive research and testing, mostly driven by the objective of figuring out what works and what doesn't. A critical part of establishing your presence online is creating a clear web development strategy. Research points out that nearly 95% of the reason people misjudge or instantly reject a website is the design aspect.

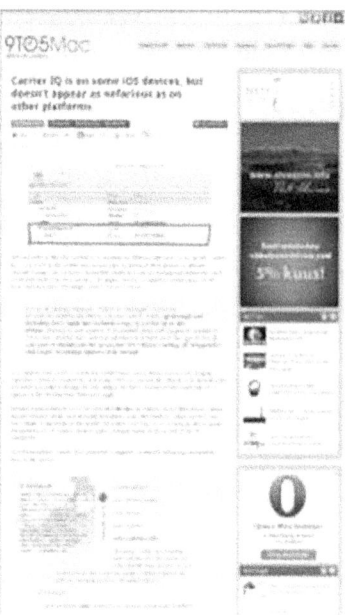

Good
vs.
Bad

A great deal of companies out there have already established a functional website and are now looking for resources on how to develop it further. One of the main problems companies face is that they've had their websites developed by a web-development company that didn't weigh in on their long-term marketing objectives nor did they pay any attention to the type of marketing they were planning to utilize. Hiring a company that helps you develop a detailed marketing plan (to deliver value long-term) and one that follows that up by creating a website matching those strategies is hands down the best way to ensure a successful outcome.

One of the main things people fail to realize is that the development of a successful website strategy involves more than simply building a website to match the brand. A much better variation of that is to start with the end goal in mind and then, as you're building the website, making sure you set in motion a number of essential components (marketing wise) that will serve as assets to your business. Assets are basically marketing strategies that make improvements to your bottom line in the form of more traffic, leads, sales, etc. Having a clear web development strategy is of the utmost importance when it comes to capturing attention and it serves as a platform for developing long-term customer relationships. You shouldn't expect a lot of success without one, and you'll find it extremely hard to convert website visitors into clients as well. However, you shouldn't let a design company convince you that this is the be-all and end-all. There are other strategic objectives marketing wise which are just as important, and we make sure to address those with equal attention to detail.

Major takeaway: Web development is merely a stepping stone (that you have to get right!) rather than a magic pill that propels a business into success.

It goes without saying that you'll need a well designed website to initiate a successful marketing campaign, and sometimes even if they're not as attracted to the front page offer they might stick around for longer because they like the design of your site. A good design encourages user engagement and will make sure you're getting the results that you want when combined with a proper marketing strategy. On the technical side of things, web development is fairly complicated as it involves the development, design, and content creation aspects. However, we tend to focus on the core value that comes with a number of different objectives/benefits:

Bringing Prospects To Their "Aha" Moment In Seconds

It's extremely hard to get a piece of the market share today if you're lacking in the design department and don't have a website which emphasizes and reflects the value you're offering within seconds. The biggest companies out there will usually have entire design teams for something as simple as a logo and data placement whilst smaller businesses have fewer resources, so they have to get it right initially.

You can outsource your work easily, but it's very important that you're dealing with a company that thoroughly understands your vision as far as what you're trying to achieve in a way that it translates to the end product. Mediocre attention to detail yields mediocre results. When a single company helps you develop an adequate marketing plan to achieve your goals, even the smallest of changes are made in a way that ultimately contributes to that. You'll also find that you usually have less than three seconds to capture a customer's attention before they move away.

The Importance Of Consistency

Consistency will not only help you increase your bottom line sales, but you'll also develop a loyal customer base for recurring sales. For that, you need a quality website that you'll be able to update on a regular basis as well as a marketing strategy to help you stay in touch with your customers. Websites are usually up on a 24/7 basis, but it's just as important to encourage website visitors to follow your updates on other mediums the likes of social media and email.

Establishing Brand Presence

As soon as a client shares his/her vision with us, we don't just look for the best way to develop a website and marketing strategy but rather what it would take to turn it into a real brand that stands a chance at competing with other brands in that respective industry.

Branding done right usually results in a lot of word-of-mouth traffic. Therefore, some of our clients are now only focused on improving their product rather than marketing it. The more your brand awareness grows, the more attention/recognition it's going to receive in that respective industry - ultimately placing you in a position where you can expand from abundance.

Your Edge Over The Competition

One of the best ways to amplify those personal recommendations that come from returning customers is by establishing a good brand presence online. Your business isn't competitive enough by merely having a great product because often times it's the ones that put their product in front of the most customers (while emphasizing value) that end up on top.

One way to instantly have an edge over the competition is by letting an experienced company take web development off your hands (paired with complex marketing strategies) and instead focus on providing as much product value as you possibly can for your business. Scroll down to the bottom to see what our typical approach to web development is.

Sluggish & Non-Responsive Websites Kill Your Customer Retention –Ensuring
Efficiency

Here's something you should keep in mind: Research has proven over and over that nearly half of all visitors are going to leave a webpage if it takes more than three seconds to load. If a page takes four seconds to load, that percentage goes up significantly. This is why you have to prioritize and ensure efficiency.

Not only is ensuring responsiveness/efficiency in website development a crucial component for retaining visitors, but this is taken a step further due to the changes in mobile surfing. In only a few years, you can expect nearly half of your overall visitors to be coming from either a smart phone or a tablet hence, you're going to need to develop a design that adapts to different screen sizes and does so as fast as possible.

Is Responsiveness All About Loading Time?

Developing a fast-loading site is actually the initial goal, although in a typical marketing strategy we usually set small goals in terms of customer engagement, such as getting every fifth visitor to sign up for the email list, for instance. This is a realistic goal that can end up contributing significantly to your bottom line profits (though a small tweak) but in order for you to keep their attention, you'll need a company that knows what it takes to preserve that attention beyond those initial few seconds. It's also important that a customer is able to see exactly the information they're looking for without having to pinch their fingers as they usually do.

You Only Have Three Seconds

If you make sure your website is optimized correctly for different devices, customers will not only reward you with their attention and more sales, but they'll also be loyal to your brand and likely mention it to their friends.

When you take into consideration that the number of people who use desktop computers to browse the internet is ever decreasing, it's of essential importance that the website adjusts for the different iOS, Android, as well as tablet devices. If you fail in that endeavor, it's going to lead to a poorer customer experience (even if your product is topnotch). For instance, if you have a blog that offers a lot of value to the reader and they plan to read through everything - why wouldn't you want them to be able to do so without having to use their fingers to pinch and swipe every few seconds? Prioritizing the user experience can be just as important as the actual product creation process, as they go hand in hand.

You're Going To Save Time

It's not only your customers that are going to be appreciative of the efforts you made to develop an adjustable version for a better experience, but you will as well. It's better to start with an optimized version from the start than have to create a separate mobile version later on because you'll need to have new code written for the different layouts and do so from scratch. Develop a rugged frame from the start because you'll only have to make small changes later on instead of having to change everything by choosing to go for the easy way out.

Considering that just about half the population of America is currently in possession of a smartphone (the percentage goes way higher when you consider the world wide population) there is no better time to start thinking about what the mobile user experience is like and devise a marketing/development strategy to accompany that. If you already have a website and you're browsing from a smartphone, ask yourself whether it's time to get a redesign and whether you're getting the full experience out of it.

Our Web Development Process Usually Goes In This Order:

1. We meet with the client (either online through email/Skype session or in person) to determine what their needs are, discuss their company culture/values as well as long-term objectives.

2. We develop a thorough/detailed marketing strategy that weighs in on the respective business's culture and objectives, and then we decide on an adequate back-end strategy. This will usually involve choosing a platform that is capable of supporting those needs.

3. Outline the whole customer experience, find ways to minimize time between the first impression and "aha" moment (for the average visitor), and determine logistics as far as where certain elements should go.

4. Give the client a realistic idea (as close to objective reality) of what to expect depending on the different strategies in question.

5. Create the first mockups. This is usually going to be an image or drawing, basically showcasing what the client can expect.

6. The review process. We focus on making sure the value your business provides is prioritized so that the different marketing channels we use later on prove to be efficient.

7. Final mockup edits.

8. We build the working version and start utilizing the different marketing strategies we agreed upon.

9. Maintenance stage. This is where we adjust the website based on customer feedback/conversions and make small tweaks consistently that improve your bottom line profits.

You can provide us with content for your websites although we have access to top-notch writers for the job at all times. We understand that each individual client has his/her own needs; hence, we take the time necessary to devise a plan that both maximizes the user experience as well as helps you meet those objectives as early on as possible.

Graphic Design

Chances are you've heard of the saying, "Never judge a book by its cover!" This is indeed a noble and powerful philosophy to carry through life, however, it certainly doesn't apply to the different behavior patterns prospects exhibit online.

The earlier you recognize how quick people are to judge (when they have nothing to lose) the more you can leverage that fact in your favor. There are lots of variables and elements of randomness that take place in the online world. Thus, you should know that on average you have only half a second before the user forms an opinion of a website. Think about it: If an ad popped up out of nowhere - how fast would you be to turn it off or pay attention? Users will judge a website just as fast even when they don't realize it's been advertised.

The first thing a good design is going to do is contribute to the trust aspect of things. Stanford recently had a study that indicated nearly 80% of all Internet users determine how credible a website is based on the design.

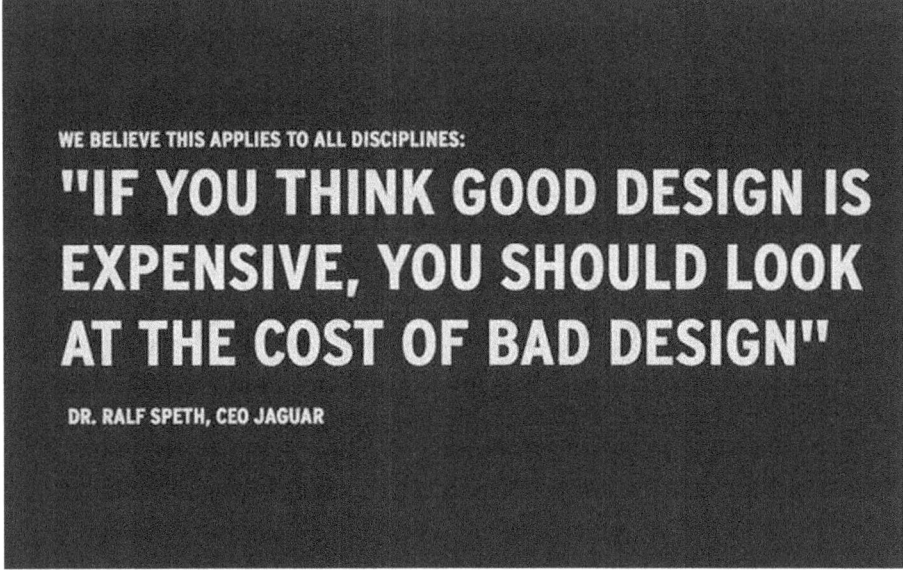

WE BELIEVE THIS APPLIES TO ALL DISCIPLINES:

"IF YOU THINK GOOD DESIGN IS EXPENSIVE, YOU SHOULD LOOK AT THE COST OF BAD DESIGN"

DR. RALF SPETH, CEO JAGUAR

In addition, if you consider that more than 80% of all Internet users take the time necessary to research a product before they purchase - that first impression you end up making online is a lot more important than the real world if you want to boost your overall profits. The way a website looks is usually the way a customer is going to feel about it. If it looks good and it emphasizes value, you can generally expect a good response. The complete opposite applies as well. Here are some of the most important facts about graphic design:

- One of the biggest epiphanies we had when testing text versus image websites in different industries and target audiences is that design is responsible for more than 90% of the first impression. Emphasizing value in terms of content is important, but the way it's presented is also considered as valuable in the customer's eyes. Even if you have the best product out there, it's going to receive poor feedback when presented with a poor design. This is especially true when it comes to building brand awareness.
- Being able to establish a positive first impression yields higher customer satisfaction and retention rates. Unless the typical customer is really desperate for access to your product because it had the right marketing or word-of-mouth beforehand, you absolutely have to leverage first impressions in your favor. Negative first impressions affect the potential a good product has by a significant margin.
- Acknowledge that a good first impression will usually last for years. There is also quite a bit of research conducted on this topic to prove just how far this theory goes. You'll notice this in very subtle things you see in real life like seeing an actor that stands out on screen in a good way and later finding out that he is quite successful. There is always time to correct a first impression (especially if you appeal to the visitor by offering them an irresistible offer that is difficult to refuse), but the extent to where you can take your business profitability wise is significantly improved by making a good first impression.

- Providing a visually pleasing experience for the average customer matters. This is especially true on the Internet where the average user is not as committed to your brand attention-wise, unless you allow them to form a good impression in a matter of seconds. This is the hard part.

Stakes Are At An All-Time High

If your business is focused on providing professional services over the long term and isn't merely selling product, making a first impression is even more important. If your whole business model is dependent on supplying businesses with high margin services, and you can't take on more than a few clients at once, you're probably aware that a single customer's positive impression can be equivalent to tens, if not even hundreds of thousands, of dollars. There is more at stake than just being on people's good side - it's there to ensure a long profitable long-term relationship with your customers.

We've been privileged to have the opportunity of working with clients in different industries and found that good design pays across the board. If you're trying to compete in a ruthless industry where a lot of your competitors are more resourceful and you're finding it hard to gain attention, this is the first step to carving out a slice of your own. If potential customers don't like your business initially, they won't bother telling you and they'll simply turn to your competition that are more than likely able to serve their needs.

Don't Just Stand Out, Be The Only One They Pay Attention To

Have you ever noticed in some industries/niches in particular there are a few select websites that just don't seem to go out of business even though thousands of others do? You'll find that the key to consistency in a competitive market is to not only make a first impression, but take the user experience to such a satisfactory level that you are literally the only one they end up paying attention to. This is why you have to ensure your marketing strategy is designed to reach those long term objectives by gradually building up to them using minor value tweaks. Graphic design is a crucial part of the process and not just an afterthought.

Behind-The-Scenes On Effective Graphic Design

You shouldn't just think of graphic design as a tool you use to make a good impression but rather as a means to help the average customer accomplish a task. This can be anything from scanning for value all the way up to categorizing your brand. You'll find that often times logos and different kinds of ads fail at helping the user accomplish that task (poor design.) Therefore, they're not nearly as effective. Some even get in the way.

There are different structural elements that go into it such as color, layout, shape, and designs. This is basically the visual representation of the value your brand provides. The most typical example of this is the Coca Cola logo that people instantly associate with the drink itself. It's important that your design cuts right to the point, allows your average visitor to find out what they wanted to know (the "aha" moment), and then helps them make a final purchase decision.

One of the biggest mistakes business owners in general end up making is they forget just how important graphic design is as a utility. They've forgotten the component of emphasizing value and making the customer feel as if you've put in the effort to make it easy for them (usually grasped in seconds.) Hence, they merely focus on the looks aspect. If you've seen one of those ads that literally make your head hurt, this is usually why. In addition, you don't just have to acknowledge that function/utility is more important than form but how to leverage that to your advantage as well.

What Can You Expect From It?

Not only is a well-made graphic design going to help you make a first impression, but it's also going to contribute to the credibility of your brand. This is something that is of essential importance if you're trying to expand to a larger level. The reality is that most business owners tend to hire designers who end up focusing on the image aspect of things while neglecting how it affects the credibility and role of a business inside a particular market.

Before you take the time to consider that, you can even look at your own shopping behavior. There's a good chance you've withdrew from purchasing a particular product merely due to the design aspect and not because you didn't feel like it was worth the investment. The reason why is because you subconsciously realized a poor design amounts to carelessness; hence, that is something you could expect when it came to their services.

When we hired designers for our team, we didn't hire them for their technical skills as much as we did for how adaptable they were between projects and their capacity in terms of understanding what works and what doesn't. The more you're involved in different marketing projects, the more you realize the same things don't work across the board. We know exactly when to follow the rules and when to break them to ensure the design doesn't interfere with your brand's image but rather enhances it.

Major takeaway: If you really want to know what are the absolute best graphic designs that are out there - it's usually the type you don't realize is there. If you take a look at the largest brands on the Internet, you'll notice the simplicity behind the visuals that represent that brand. Though these visuals have been carefully tested and designed. Consequently, the majority of people don't acknowledge them.

Making People Associate Real-Life Situations With Your Brand

Branding is more than making people remember your business or logo. It's really about developing a symbol that people will instantly associate as you, so try and translate that into real life situations. If you simply say "soda" you'll likely have a few brands pop into your head instantly. This comes as a direct result of good branding. If you want to make a name for your brand in a particular industry, you have to take it to a point where people will associate the core of that industry to your brand name/value.

Not only will you get more people remembering what your brand is all about, but it's also going to become recognizable in an instant in your market. This is basically the first step to establishing a successful presence in an industry that is regarded as competitive.

Are Logos That Important?

Although they don't represent the big picture, a logo can be crucial to that first impression we mentioned earlier and you have to make it as simple as possible. It's definitely wise to have branding experts work with experienced designers when it comes to making your logo because there are lots of subtleties going into it.

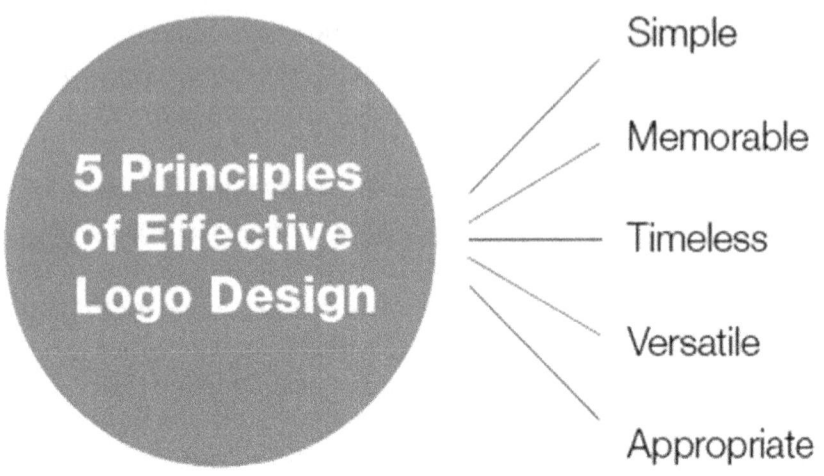

- A logo should be a visual representation of a brand that looks good in every size. Think of the Nike logo: It looks good on a small shoe but it also looks good when placed on a New York City billboard. A logo can be in the form of a symbol, text, or a combination of both.
- Often times the first impression is ruined because a customer can tell straight away whether someone has put the effort in to designing a logo that actually represents that image the brand in question is trying to portray. They can see right through that.
- If you're not trying to build a major brand and simply want to focus on updating a very select target audience with specific information, a logo is usually not as important as making sure you emphasize the value. Depending on your specific goals, you should know whether a logo is necessary off the bat.

How Far Can Branding Be Taken With Graphic Design?

You should know that the graphic design aspect (considering it's backed up by an excellent marketing strategy) is going to help make impressions in a lot more places than the main website.

For instance, if you're operating a real store you'll likely use it there, on your website, your eBay account, promotional events, commercials, media buys, etc. The logo in particular is going to show up on just about everything that is viewed as a part of the company.

Saving Time With People Who Understand What It Takes

If you're dealing with marketing consultants who don't also provide you with access to well- trained graphic designers that will design a logo necessary to meet your marketing objectives, it's the same as hiring a designer that is unaware of the image you're trying to portray in a customer's eyes.

Graphic design is a lot more than being skilled in Photoshop as it's a crucial factor that can determine whether a business is going to be successful or fade away in the coming years. Getting started with us will ensure everything is taken care of you in this time consuming process so that you can spend more time working on delivering/improving actual product value.

Lead Generation

Attracting High Quality Leads And Turning Them Into Loyal Customers

We don't just specialize in creating an efficient brand framework, but based on your long-term objectives, we structure everything in a way that puts you in a position to attract qualified leads consistently.

When it comes to the hows and whys of attracting quality leads, it's actually not that complicated. We've built up an entire database of reliable websites; we have hands-on experience with the best of advertising options and sometimes partner up with other marketing agencies to achieve a single objective.

The most well known concept of lead generation is to target specific audiences, make them fill out their information, and then sell that information to businesses that have an interest in selling to the leads. However, we tend to focus on attracting leads to your brand on a personal level and helping you build a database of your own so you can market to people who are actually interested and want to stay engaged over the long term.

Which Businesses Benefit The Most From Lead Generation?

There are very few exceptional industries that don't require leads for sustainability or ones that wouldn't benefit from leads at all. Even sites where people usually don't end up spending money, such as video streaming websites, could utilize lead generation to stay in touch with their visitors, and lead generation is especially important where volumes are low but margins are high. For instance, if you're offering a very exclusive service and can only take on a few clients at a time - you'll likely benefit from a few leads that are interested than you would from thousands that you have to persuade over and over.

- Statistics indicate that nearly 80% of all leads marketers acquire don't end up converting. Our goal here is to attract the type of leads that fall into the 20% bracket, and one of the main ways we ensure that is through careful targeting and a detailed nurturing process.
- The lack of appropriate call-to-action in a follow up email series usually results in a decrease of readership and product interest. We know exactly when to sell, how to provide value, and do so without being obvious.
- We take the time necessary to test the efficiency of a landing page and usually end up creating tens of different variations to end up with one that produces the most favorable results.
- As you're launching different campaigns, you'll usually attract different customers; consequently, it's important to adjust current landing pages or create new ones.

Reasons Why Your Strategy Didn't Work:

You Didn't Emphasize Value The Right Way

This is usually the case with small business owners because they forget about the component of empathy, and this is not because they don't have anything valuable to offer but rather it all seems so obvious in their eyes. It's easy to get caught up in the hype of your own product or become biased to the emotions of first time viewers; hence, you really have to know how to outline the benefits they'll be getting directly and where.

You Didn't Set-Up Funnels The Right Way

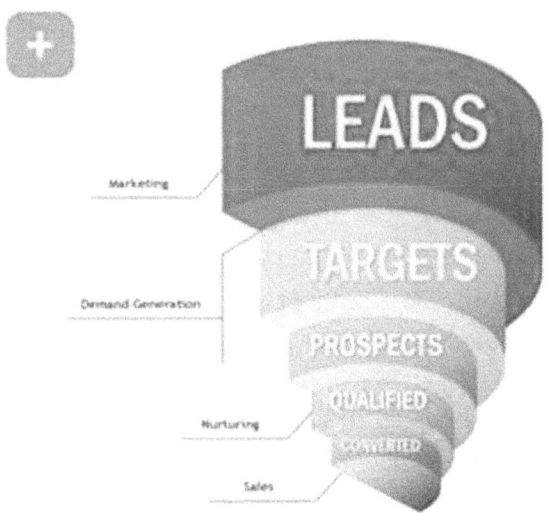

If you're operating a store on a very busy street, usually the only thing that you have to do is open your doors and wait for the business to come to you. However, if you take this approach online, more often than not, you won't get those desirable results.

You can literally have a product that outshines everything your competition is currently offering (at a great rate as well), but if you don't know how to convert leads or have an effective system that allows you to reach them afterwards - you don't stand a chance. We know exactly what it takes to make a visitor of your landing page perceive your product value the same way as you do, except we do it in a matter of seconds.

You're Not Dealing With The Right People

Often times you'll hear marketers emphasizing the importance of targeted traffic, but this goes a lot longer when it comes to lead generation. It's not that different from going out into the real world and expecting everyone to like you and respect you for who you are - it's merely a fantasy. Some people will resonate with what you have to offer, and others will be put off instantly.

However, you can have a real advantage if you know how to present that value in a most favorable manner so that people who see the value in it are instantly hooked and keep coming back for more. Often times, getting a few clients who take your work seriously and end up bringing you thousands of dollars every month can be better than dozens or hundreds that don't pay you as much and take up more of your time. The hard part is finding those leads. This is why presentation/impressions matter, and they have to cut to the core initially.

You Didn't Utilize More Than One Marketing Channel

There are lots of proven ways to attract quality leads, and we make sure to devise a strategy based on your long-term expectancy and objectives. For instance, if you're looking for ways to build brand awareness on an existing site the obvious answer is to establish presence on different social media outlets or provide a lot of value through video/content marketing. On the other hand, if all you need are a few targeted clients in your local area that you know are going to boost your bottom line profits, there are appropriate and subtler ways to go about achieving that as well.

Our Process To Ensuring Consistency In Quality Leads: Starting With The End Goal In Mind

We understand that the process of generating quality leads takes a lot of effort and isn't merely setting up a landing page and sending out emails. It's important to develop a thorough, detailed, and timely process for the follow up.

Some of the main aspects which have to be addressed initially include mediums that you'll be using to attract those leads to your landing page, getting them from a good first impression to an "aha" moment (when they realize what you're offering clearly), and converting that curiosity into a purchase decision. These are all complicated in their own right, and different rules apply to different businesses. Hence, you should contact us for the best approach for your situation.

Prioritizing Value Over Sales Copy

The best way to know what this means is to put yourself in your customers' shoes. You have to know what they're thinking, how they behave, what their fears are, as well as their motives for buying. As you gather more information about the average customer who ends up on your landing page, the whole process of giving them what they need (providing value) becomes a whole lot easier.

Sometimes even the most compelling offer isn't going to resonate with a certain target audience. The last thing you want to do with lead generation is be ignorant of these crucial details in terms of your customers' wants/needs and emotional responses.

Often times people offer a free consultation, and this is especially the case when it comes to offering quality services. However, you have to think of the way an average customer is going to interpret that. Even if they have nothing to lose and everything to gain by purchasing your product, overselling it can put them off. This is why it's important to structure your lead generation campaigns in a way that you prioritize value but not miss out on the subtleties that goes into the creation of a profitable marketing campaign.

Requesting Their Information

The important thing to emphasize here is that you have to frame it the right way. It's actually useful for you to gather up as much information as you can, but you have to know how to do it right. Otherwise, it's going to put a person off instantly. The more you're asking, the less you're going to get.

A great way to think about lead generation is as a win-win situation in which you're exchange value for the information they give you. For instance, if you're giving away software and they end up liking it (instant value) your follow up can be as simple as offering a feature upgrade, and you won't have any problem making sales. And **the more information that you're looking to get, the more value you'll have to provide in return**.

We usually keep track of basic information such as name, location, email, time spent on the website, overall responsiveness, etc., and we can draw conclusions from that. Simply think of the average person that would find value in your product: What are their main problems and pain points you can address? Issues can be very personal (things people won't open up about in real life) such as wanting to fix their teeth, lose weight, remove moles/tattoos, whiten teeth, etc. The more personal it is, the more universal it is.

Keeping Track Of Everything

The last thing a professional does is to rely on luck and shots in the dark. An effective strategy combines a solution to a very personal problem (or value of any kind) along with hard, statistical data. You have to keep track of things like lead quality, history of contact, dates, origins, landing pages, sales, and so on. Tracking is important from the minute they visit your page and is certainly one of the key components to an effective lead generation strategy.

Ensuring A Return On Investment

Our objective when trying to meet our client's demands is not to generate a massive amount of leads but rather attract leads that are interested in their product and keep coming back for more. We focus on cost per sale and things that emphasize lead quality.

Reviewing/Adjusting Based On Progress

Our main objective isn't to merely attract quality leads, sell once, and let go of them. We're more focused on building brands so that these people keep coming back while simultaneously attracting more leads from the same channels. Often times there are elements of randomness that we didn't predict from the start; thus, we end up making adjustments. This is a stage where we're focused on two things mostly: maintenance and expansion. We keep track of all progress, fix issues as they come up, and keep testing when needed.

Following Up And Nurturing Leads

One of the biggest problems people face when getting started with lead generation on their own is that they fail to get instant results. This is mostly because they're approaching it from the wrong mindset and instead of nurturing those leads to ultimately end up with more bottom line profits, all they're focused on is the instant sale. Some of those leads will definitely go for it immediately (assuming you have a compelling offer), but it does take time to build up trust before people pull out their credit cards - even if you have value.

Weighing In On Your Long Term Goals

There isn't a single method out there that is consistency reliable for all customers. Furthermore we take the time necessary to consider your specific goals and propose the best strategy, which will ensure long-term value/consistency for your business.

Often times the small changes that are made can result in a dozen new customers for your business, which can significantly affect your bottom line for the better. I'm sure it feels great to walk into your office on a regular Monday morning and find out that you've made sales, acquired new leads, and potential new customers are calling you.

Email Marketing

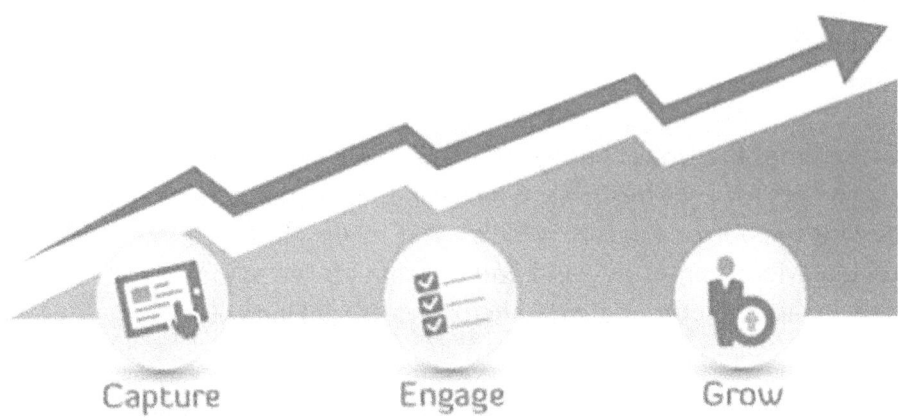

Capture   Engage   Grow

Email marketing is an essential component of an effective marketing strategy that can help increase your sales, attract quality leads, and increase customer retention. It's in your best interest to get as personal as you can with your customers; thus, email marketing is one of the mediums that allow you to do that. When done right, email marketing can work wonders for your bottom line profits. Here are some of the main reasons why you should consider developing an email marketing strategy (even if you don't plan to use it as a primary medium.)

It Doesn't Burn Through Your Budget

In comparison to a lot of paid marketing strategies out there, email marketing is among the least expensive when you pay attention to detail. If your main marketing strategy revolves around media buying (which usually isn't as targeted) you can usually expect to spend 5-10x as much as you would for a comparable quality of leads.

It's good that you get immediate feedback because you don't have to print things out and put them out there in the real world. The main investments are for the research, backend software, and campaign creation for follow-ups. The Direct Marketing Association recently proved that a well-developed email marketing strategy can yield as much as 4,000% ROI.

Location Is Irrelevant

The majority of email users read emails on a daily basis (90%+) and this is a real advantage over buying ads on media because the engagement is high and you're not limited to a particular geographical region. As long as they have Internet access, they'll usually end up reading your follow-ups if they're appealing enough (which we make sure they are!).

No Wait Time For Feedback

One major advantage to email marketing is that in addition to the high engagement rate and global reach, you also don't have to wait a lot to see a result. Conversion rates are through the roof with effective email marketing and this is mainly because it only takes a few clicks before they end up landing on your "Checkout" page.

Reach People Who Want To Hear From You

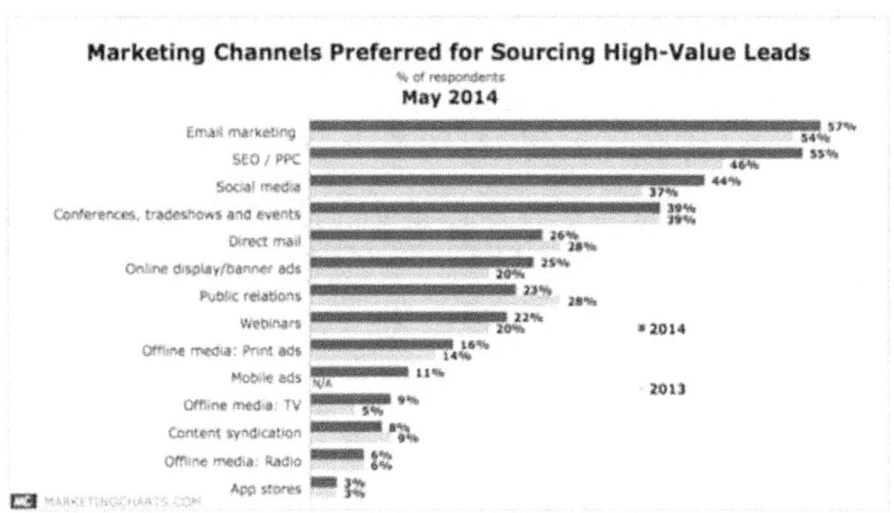

There's a decent chance you're already reading a newsletter from someone, and you've been doing so for years, or you have a favorite marketer who you just know will learn a lot from, so you end up opening their emails even when you know you won't purchase.

When you utilize our lead generation services, we basically develop strategic objectives to reach a certain target audience and send leads your way that are actually interested in what you have to say/offer and will increase your bottom line profits instead of having to deal with time wasters.

Often times marketing consultants prioritize conversion rates ahead of actual quality of leads; hence, even when they send out attention-grabbing emails, they don't end up selling as much. The good thing is that with email marketing you have the opportunity to build a list of people who are eager to hear from you and build a database of extremely loyal customers.

Stay In Touch With Customers (Or Prospects) Even If You Don't Sell

All business owners don't necessarily utilize email marketing as a means to get instant sales, but often times they'll use it to increase user engagement on the site and make them more responsive to the content they're putting out. **Here's what you should remember**: Most people on the Internet will end up purchasing something, one way or another. You want to be there when they are ready to make a purchase and your company will be one they choose once they're ready? It's obviously your the brand they're already familiar with and they have gotten a lot of value from you just by staying subscribed to your email list.

It's Personal

Depending on what you're trying to achieve, we can optimize your messages to be personal and greet people by their name. Email marketing technology allows you to use the prospect's information you get at sign up (name, surname, city, etc.) directly inside the email. People also don't usually hand out their personal email to everyone, and with a smart strategy you can definitely go a long way.

You Can Divide Campaigns

It's wise to develop different campaigns for different target audiences, which will allow you to send more personalized emails, promote specific products, or reward current customers. Relevance is key here, and segmentation helps with getting it right.

Track/Measure Everything

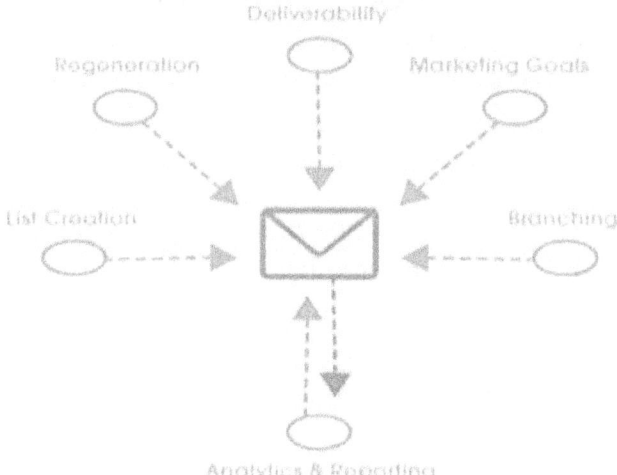

You'll have access to just about everything in relation to your email marketing campaign and not just the leads you gathered and emails you've sent out. For instance, you'll know how many emails were opened, who opened them, who clicked, and the links they chose to click on. This will allow you to further segregate data and make small tweaks to improve engagement.

Forwarding

If you're sharing highly valuable information (as we'll encourage you) you'll find that a lot of your prospects end up forwarding the email. We'll provide you with a list of people who actually forwarded your email. These are the best leads of all.

Leverage On Impulsive Buyers

Keeping in mind that well over 65% of online shoppers have made an instant purchase decision as a result of an email marketing campaign, the first thing that comes to mind when it comes to mass impulsive buying online is email marketing. Think about it: If you were considering going on a vacation somewhere, you had the money saved up and a travel agency suddenly sent you an email full of interesting promotions within your budget – wouldn't you be tempted? If they're familiar with your brand and you've warmed them up properly, the right call to action can result in a lot of success.

Up-Selling Is Easier Than Ever

We use segmentation to create lists of people who have already purchased from you and then carefully let them know about other services of yours that they're potentially interested in. You'll not only get those initial sales, but you might even end up making most of your money through up-sells on the back end.

Not Hard To Maintain

It does take at least a few hours to write an email worth sharing with a mass audience, and one you can expect a decent conversion on, but you would rather focus on the product value itself, and let us maintain your email campaigns as you grow. We also make sure our emails are optimized for mobile; only around 10% are, and this is a staggering fact considering that nearly 50% of all emails are opened on smartphones within 15 minutes.

Mistakes That Kill An Email Marketing Strategy

Here's a fact that will blow your mind: Nearly 90% of all email that a person receives lands in the spam category. One of the main things we focus on as part of an effective email marketing strategy is that our client's emails don't end up being categorized as spam. This is usually a complicated process, but we've already established relationships with different service providers and have a number of tricks up our sleeve to ensure your messages make it to where they are supposed it. It's also not uncommon for legit emails to be labeled as spam, and there really isn't a way to ensure 100% of your emails are going to end up in the inbox folder.

- Even if your lead generation strategy is effective and conversions are through the roof, you might still experience problems with deliverability and segmentation. This is what we refer to as a "hot mess" as you have all the proof it works, but the mechanics aren't as laid out as they should be.
- Adequate segmentation helps you differentiate between the people who've already purchased some of your products. For instance, you can make a list of people who purchased one of your mid-priced products within the last 2 weeks.
- Not testing enough is one of the biggest mistakes business owners make when it comes to marketing. In our lead generation strategy, we emphasize the importance of attracting leads that are very interested in what you have to offer--these are the ones you should be focused on. Keep in mind that different lead groups are going to respond to offers differently, so it's best not to take shots in the dark by sending the same thing to everyone, and instead focus in on the subtleties and specifics.
- If you haven't developed a well-organized list that allows you to keep track of how you're doing, what your pain points are, and what you can improve instantly--you aren't doing it right. The worst

thing you could do is to play a guessing game, as this leads to nowhere, unless you rely on getting lucky which isn't consistent. Our strategy involves the organization of your entire database, tweaks/improvements, massive testing, and the creation of systems for you to use over the long term.

Know What Your Customer Are Thinking To Engage Them

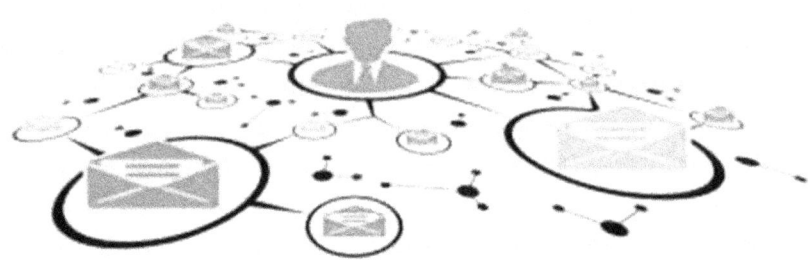

We come from the mindset of reaching out to a single average customer. We're basically looking for ways to find out what your average customer is like, what they consider as valuable, and what they respond to on a personal/emotional level. In order for us to do that, in addition to thorough market research, we make sure to utilize powerful reporting tools (which give you all you need to know about a target audience), information on your average audience that ends up opening your emails, what they usually do in response (forward or open links) and people who have chosen to unsubscribe. Even if you have a massive amount of people unsubscribing, you'll usually be able to see patterns and quickly make improvements to baby step out of it.

Our Process Of Creating An Effective Email Marketing Strategy:

1. Thorough research on how the market functions, your competition, and different industry trends in order to determine an effective marketing strategy.

2. Determining what your goals are and realistic results you can expect over the long term so you can start working towards them.

3. Information about the average user. This is really what binds it all together because if you know what the average user on your website responds to or resonates with, it's extremely easy to give it to him/her. Demographics are a major factor as well.

4. Determine which strategies your competitors are using and what their main weaknesses are.

5. Identifying real value you can provide long term by researching the pain points that are present throughout your market and people are trying to address.

6. Creating new streams of revenue in the form of up sells or improving products/services.

7. Reporting progress to you and making adjustments based on that.

8. Create an email marketing calendar that includes follow-up emails as well as long-term business objectives you're trying to reach.

9. Providing our customers a peace of mind knowing that they're dealing with the most experienced of marketing consultants and letting them focus on product value instead of mechanics.

Search Marketing

It doesn't take long to realize how important search marketing is for your business, and sometimes it can be considered the lifeblood of your marketing strategy. Plenty of amazing products and service offerings have failed for the sole reason that they weren't placed in front of the right people; therefore, they were in no position to reach their sales potential. Retaining a presence on social media and putting a number of marketing strategies in place is essential, but making sure you're visible on all major search engines in the right way is crucial as well, this is where we step in.

In order for you to save money, it's important to make sure you're dealing with a marketing agency that has plenty of reference experience in terms of what works when bringing your product to the forefront. Search marketing is a lot more complicated than selecting keywords and ranking websites because the placements have to both reach out to a target audience as well as reflect your brand values the right way.

Often times agencies will burn through your budget as they're experimenting, and this is especially true if they're inexperienced when it comes to highly competitive industries. The key here is to ensure a steady return on investment for your company and to put you in a position where you can experiment from a safe starting point.

The bottom line to effective search marketing is that it's among the most time consuming activities, and it requires a lot of expertise in the area to ensure a desirable result. A person lacking the knowledge necessary to make a product stand out and attract attention from the right people can easily blow through a budget and have nothing to show for it. Our mission is to provide efficient search marketing services for quality products/services that have the potential of expansion and prioritize long term results over instant gratification. We use our experienced team members to get everything going for you so that you have more time to focus on developing your product.

Disadvantage To Keep In Mind

What you should be aware of is that effective search marketing isn't done overnight and that it takes time to build a solid reputation. This statement goes even farther if you're in a very competitive market, and sometimes it can take months to fully develop a strategy for expansion. We're always trying to reach for the highest level possible and know exactly what it takes for you to save both time as well as money.

Time management is a priority for us because we're trying to come up with a strategy that allows you to expand and see results long term whilst making sure your costs are kept as low as possible. It's important that we communicate frequently as a lot of times we end up making adjustments in the process.

As mentioned, there are various forms of search marketing (both free and paid) hence it's in your best interest to let an experienced team devise a careful strategic approach for it. Depending on your budget and product quality, we can predict how long it's going to take for you to see your ideal results.

Time Is Of The Essence – How To Hold An Edge Over Your Competition

You're not only at an advantage from a product development standpoint when you decide to hire us (because you can spend more time on building your business, but you'll basically have an edge over the competition who likely don't have an efficient marketing team to work on their marketing strategy. We've been successful in the business for years and made it through the roughest times because we always provide quality, value and generated long-term results for our clients. Even experienced marketers can benefit from our services.

Pay-per-click, or PPC marketing, is one of the most well known segments of search marketing and one you're likely considering if you're trying to ensure your business takes off fast. WordStream recently did a study indicating nearly 65% of all "buying intent" keyword traffic out there goes to the sponsored listings and 35% to the organic rankings. Most people are unaware that they're visiting a sponsored website, and this is a real advantage as it brings you to the forefront instantly, although there are plenty of variables taking place there.

Optimizing your website for organic search rankings usually takes a lot more as you'll have to build up a brand of relevance and authority in the search engine's eyes, and this can take months, if not even years. The general thing to remember is that there is a lot more going into it than targeting keywords and gathering up links to a website.

You Can't Rely On PPC Tools Exclusively

Years of experience showed us that there are always certain marketing touch-points out there, which have to be addressed, and ones that are relevant to the average customer's experience. This is something that PPC tools will simply not show you, and often times it's a shot in the dark unless you're prepared to pay an astronomical amount of money.

We look deep into problems that the average user in your market is facing, gather up data to support that, and create an approach that targets both direct and indirect keywords for placement. In addition, we utilize a number of different marketing channels to ensure customer retention such as combining this with email marketing and social media. It's not uncommon for a customer to visit your website, decide to subscribe instead of purchasing right away, and then purchase your product later on. We realized that commercial intent keywords are effective, but when people are indirectly searching for solutions to problems they can't articulate well, it's something we can definitely work with as well.

If you're exclusively relying on technical information that has already been out there for years, but don't know how to fiercely target real problems your clients are facing and present yourself as the best solution, it's best to address that as early as possible. We also design our marketing campaigns and websites in a way that promotes long-term interaction with a prospect because our experience has shown that people like to interact with a brand at least a few times prior to making a purchase. An interaction can be anything from seeing a well-placed ad to giving you their email.

A large part of building an efficient PPC marketing campaign is knowing how to target the right prospects and making the most out of your budget so that you get the maximum return on investment. This always requires a unique approach because if you're selling extremely expensive services for instance, you'll likely need only a few targeted visits to attract a high-margin customer. Sometimes a well placed ad on a single keyword that drives fewer (but targeted) people to your website than another which gives you a lot more exposure can actually give you the most return on your investment.

Smart Strategy Development Based On Your Long-Term Budget/Goals

It's not wise to settle on a single marketing budget when you're starting out without continuously make adjustments based on your ROI. As mentioned earlier, PPC is not merely a numbers game but it still requires a smart approach. For instance, you might think that spending $200 a week on advertising is nothing, but over the course of a year that adds up to more than $10,000 in ad spending. Sometimes it could actually be better to spend more initially which will give you an accurate idea of what to expect and then stretching the winners out over the long term.

Providing Access To Your Ideal Clients Rather Than Time Wasters

Google is the largest search engine out there that we spend the most time experimenting with and getting results from. They're basically providing us with a mix of different media we can use for advertising, and we put all our efforts into leveraging that to our client's advantage. The key tactic behind how we achieve efficiency for lead generation is simply relevance. Relevance can be displayed in different forms such as a good first impression, making ads that deeply resonate with what their thoughts are, providing solutions without overselling, and exclusively targeting people who are in need of the value your product/services provide.

We also back everything up with advanced tracking technology that basically allows us to see how different marketing channels perform so we can emphasize and put more attention on those in the future. We'll basically be able to tell whether natural or paid visits generate the most desirable behavior in a customer, what your main sticking points/flaws are, and how to lower a prospect's time of reaction (before the "aha" moment) once they land on your site.

Marketers usually debate whether a shorter keyword is worth the additional placement cost considering it's going to bring them a decent amount of traffic, over a longer keyword that is cheaper but doesn't provide as much exposure. There really is no definite answer to that because as soon as you've figured out the main pain points a customer in your market is facing and have the tools to research ways to combine that with your marketing strategy, you'll have a decent starting point and an idea of what needs to be done.

After a number of years of continuously running campaigns across different markets and trying out a lot of things, we found out that even the best devised strategies can become a victim of their own success. For instance, being consistent with PPC marketing is one of the toughest things to do because if you managed to replicate success a few times it can actually give you a false sense of security. It's in your best interest to focus on building a core audience through a number of different marketing channels so that your brand is set up for organic growth over the long term.

This is why we make sure to give you the absolute best of search marketing placement strategies for your business, and we do so in conjunction with a number of different marketing channels.

There Is No Final Destination Point

Since it is very difficult to determine what the search engine algorithms are for organic traffic, there is more consistency in PPC marketing, even though you have to keep in mind that this is something that will require constant adjustment. You will rarely have to do an entire overhaul in terms of strategy, but carefully tracking your performance and making changes to the ad buys constantly is important.

We always make sure your ads are relevant to the prospect by doing massive research and encourage them to take action whilst stretching out your budget to go as far as possible. Even if you have campaigns that are currently doing well, there is still improvement that can be done.

Putting Your Brand In The Center Of It All

Being that we're likely going to end up placing your website in front of thousands of relevant prospects, even if they don't decide to visit your website instantly and purchase, the fact that you have that presence is what's going to ensure that they keep you in mind over the long term. This is one of the main advantages to search marketing as it increases your brand awareness and that initial cost will eventually prove useful.

Social Media Management

The influential reach of social media stretches far beyond connecting people as it's becoming an increasingly important part of modern-day purchase decisions. People are constantly on the lookout for reinforcement and social proof prior to making a decision hence retaining presence on social media could increase your business tenfold.

When you consider just how fast the smartphone market is blowing up all over the world and the fact that most people use their smartphones for social media exclusively, leaving it out of your marketing strategy is no longer an option. People make decisions a lot quicker now and you can easily leverage this to your advantage by knowing exactly how to give them what they want. For instance, if someone is considering staying at a hotel, they'll likely look into the Facebook page for pictures and prior guest reviews. This helps them reinforce their decision and is usually the determining factor.

If we only go back a decade ago, when people wanted to purchase something, word of mouth was usually the best way to reinforce a decision. Otherwise, they'd have to go to a nearby shop and try their luck. At the present moment, there is so much information on just about every product out there that it becomes overwhelming. It saves time for the end user but the actual work that goes in behind-the-scenes, which will allow you to establish a page that actually reinforces purchase decision, is the hard part.

If you're trying to establish a name for yourself or build a brand from nothing, it's absolutely necessary for you to partake in social media to a degree. We're here to help you leverage your online presence by carefully researching the mechanics of your market and putting together a strategy that will help you draw attention and encourage action as a result.

People have so much trust in a recommendation made via social media that it's easily on par with word of mouth advertising. Not to mention that with the right strategy, you can quickly reach a target audience and build a brand from the ground up in a matter of months. Here are some of the more obvious benefits to utilizing social media for your business, before we get to our unique approach.

You Need It For SEO

There is a lot more to search engine marketing than simply picking out keywords and sending backlinks to a page. Not only will a great marketing strategy for social media increase the necessary social proof and provide you with a platform upon which you can build your brand, but it also reinforces the proof search engines need to rank your brand.

As your brand starts growing, you'll automatically notice people talking about it on their own websites, and what will usually happen is that the social media pages we've established from the start are going to end up on the first page results along with your main website.

Another major benefit to social media that promotes engagement is the fact that your target audience will be looking forward to updates. This can be something as simple as sharing discounts, new offers, creating events, or anything of value. It's key to establishing long-term engagement and attaining the recognition that comes with that.

Plenty Of Room To Get Creative

There are some obvious questions you'll have to ask yourself that go beyond offering value such as whether you'll be getting the engagement you looked forward to and if you'll end up spending more than you're supposed to for subpar results. The good thing about social media is that you can basically try out a number of different ideas that have the potential of bringing results and because it's so engaging by nature, you'll instantly know what you did right and which pain points your business has to address so you can strategize further. All social media pages get the same treatment initially; the only difference is whether you'll set everything up in a way that allows you to grow over time or not.

It's Personal

Regular methods of advertising that most people can think of are usually in the form of billboards and posters plastered throughout different parts of the city. The downside to advertising of this kind is that it's not personal (unless it addresses/promotes personal issues), and social media is the opposite of that.

You're basically giving the privilege of interacting with your prospects in a personal way, as they'll usually end up liking things that they resonate with the most. It not only increases brand awareness but loyalty as well. As of 2014 social media actually overtook porn as the main activity on the Internet and more than 70% of adults in the U.S. are already on Facebook.

One of our main marketing objectives when it comes to social media is to build your brand up in a way that encourages the development of a relationship with your prospects/clients rather than trying to push sales at all times. We use an arsenal of tools to help you build up that interaction and gather up a lot of information in terms of what they're after so you can give it to them strategically.

Your Brand Goes A Lot Longer

You can literally build an entire brand up online without spending as much as you would on regular advertising methods. We'll show you a number of ways you can leverage that instant feedback you're getting which saves you invaluable time you can be using to further develop your product.

We basically set everything up for consistency and long-term value rather than focusing on instant gratification and letting your brand depend on sudden spikes in traffic. It's important to think of your brand as a human that interacts with others through the Internet and this is especially true when it comes to social media. People are very hostile to direct selling approaches on social media; hence, it takes a lot of strategizing and thorough research to build a platform for consistent growth.

Your Reputation Goes Up And So Does Your Authority

Your agenda is clearly visible through the updates you end up leaving on social media hence this is one of the best ways to build a reputation as a company of value. Facebook and Twitter make it easy for customers to share everything you've tweeted. Therefore, your brand awareness goes up instantly if you're known for putting out relevant content. This helps build up that core audience which is absolutely mandatory for start-ups and is one of the keys to a successful marketing campaign.

It Makes Selling Easier

As soon as we've established your brand as a valuable one and gained the trust of a core audience, selling becomes one of the easiest things in the world for the mere fact that it feels natural.

Do you ever notice how certain brands can easily make a lot of sales without trying hard because they've offered so much in the past whilst others keep hammering it out with advertising and end up with mediocre results? It's absolutely mandatory that you solidify your stand in a particular industry so when the time comes to sell, your prospects are so warm that it becomes nothing more than a formality.

Large Sharks Don't Have An Astronomical Advantage

People will usually gravitate towards what they feel is the most valuable thing for them at a particular point in time, not which company has the largest advertising budget. In the real world, it's extremely hard to compete with retailers that already have an established presence and large marketing budgets, but social media gives you a fresh start in the sense that there will always be a core audience interested in what you have to offer. You can penetrate your competitor's turf by letting us design a strategic marketing plan which gives you the platform to get going and eventually outgrow them.

Benefits To Utilizing Our Social Media Management Services

We're confident enough to take on even the most competitive and ferocious industries out there. Our role is to help you maximize the core engagement you're getting, raise your brand awareness on a local or global scale, and help you get a piece of the cake. We only work with clients who understand the importance of core value and user engagement to help them set the platform for long-term success.

We Prioritize Your Company Culture And Vision

Understanding this is what's most important to us and the things that assist us in making the right decisions for you. We're mostly interested in working with brands that are in it for the long run and understand core product value thus we have to know the mechanics of your brand inside out.

We do a lot of research on your customer's pain points, wants/needs, responsiveness and engagement so we can utilize that later on when crafting a marketing strategy. Schedule a Skype call to see what we can bring to the table.

We're Very Skilled Communicators

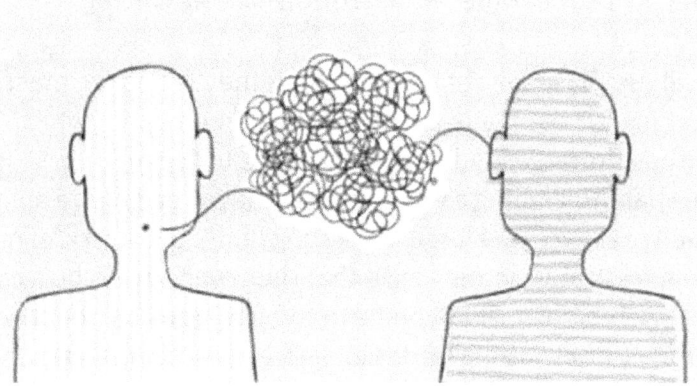

We use a number of different platforms for communication (if the brand is not located in our area) so we can communicate coherently as we're devising and implementing the strategies. It's of absolute importance to us to take full responsibility for the way your brand's values are represented and projected onto the public; hence, we have to communicate as much as possible.

We have different departments that are focused on accomplishing tasks from our marketing objectives and we certainly consider it an advantage having people from different marketing backgrounds working on one common goal. We will discuss everything thoroughly, update you on progress, send you suggestions, and ultimately allow you to have more time to work on improving product.

Tackle Objectives Easier With The Right Strategies

We don't have a single business model that works universally, but what we do have is a lot of experience in terms of what works and what doesn't, so it won't take long for us to evaluate and devise a marketing plan to match your specific needs.

Often times competing marketing agencies utilize a uniform plan across all their clients, and this is something we avoid doing, not because we're insecure about it, but rather because we understand different markets require different approaches. We're constantly on the lookout for ways to put our clients in a position where they can maximize their earning potential and allow them to bring their strength to the forefront while minimizing the pain points.

Engage Your Core Audience On A Deeper Level

In addition to looking for ways to understand your brand and company culture to the core, we also put our efforts in understanding what it takes to draw attention in your market and help empathize with your target audience. Being able to relate to your customers on a deep level doesn't just involve a good understanding of what their problems are but also what the subtleties of the market are, whether we're using their language and bringing value in a way that they can resonate with. This helps us actively communicate with your audience and establish you as the authority. Attracting traffic/attention is one thing, but retaining it and boosting engagement is another.

Strategic Plans That Work And Save Time

The reason why we've received a lot of success in the past is mainly due to our ability to implement those strategic plans and set our clients on a path to success for decades to come. We don't exclusively focus on marketing strategies that we know will work based on our research, but we make sure these strategies are a reflection of your individual business objectives. As a result, those marketing objectives are quickly met, and you as the business owner end up saving a lot of time while simultaneously being the opportunity to focus on improving your product.

Video Creation And Marketing

A Third Of All Online Activity Is Spent On Video Content

Among the top reasons you should consider implementing a large-scale video marketing strategy for your business is the fact that over 75% of all internet traffic for 2017 is projected to be about videos. Video marketing is an essential part of our marketing strategy and there are lots of advantages to getting started early:

Access To A Broad Audience

It goes without mentioning that YouTube is among the most visited sites on the Internet; moreover, your presence there is essential. When done right, a video marketing strategy could become one of your main sources for lead generation as there's a high possibility your videos are going to be noticed and shared.

People don't just watch videos for entertainment, but do so for answers as well. Google is still the leading search engine when it comes to people looking for answers, but YouTube comes in second, even ahead of Bing. This means that with an adequately executed strategy, your potential for reaching your target audiences increases exponentially.

Videos Are Engaging

There is unlimited creative potential when it comes to making videos, and you can take it way beyond the regular video promotions. People find videos engaging, and a lot of them are going to leave invaluable feedback (without realizing it) that you can directly use for improvement.

Branding Made Easy

Video is key to increasing brand awareness, and this is mainly because they get that extra feel for the core value your products/services are there to offer. People can tell whether a company is reputable based on subtleties such as the way of presenting, voice, music, general vibe, and the social proof that comes with it.

Video is not only key when introducing new products to the market but in order to help a prospect make a purchasing decision. Major retailers have conducted research indicating that more than 90% of people who saw a video about a product they planned on purchasing actually helped them make that decision. There is also the possibility of a video going viral, although we tend to focus on putting out valuable content for a target audience and making it grow gradually.

Think about it. **People remember...**

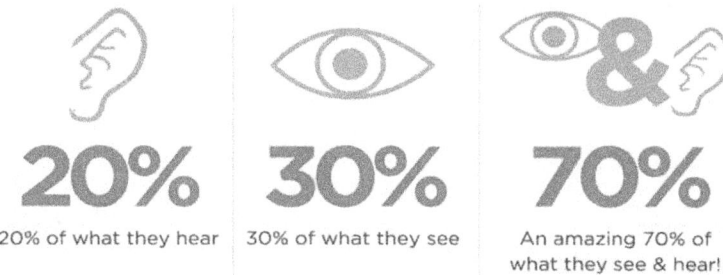

20%	30%	70%
20% of what they hear	30% of what they see	An amazing 70% of what they see & hear!

The impact video has on a prospect in comparison to regular text is enormous. Forrester Research points out that a single minute of video (assuming it's done right) can make up for thousands of words worth of content. However, when combined with other marketing channels as well as a number of value conveyers--there is very little resistance prospects display if they're considering buying a product. It's basically instant value.

What We Aim For In Terms Of Content

We find that the best way to bring in leads and build a target audience that grows over the long term is to make content that is both entertaining as well as informative. The balance between the two is key because if you lean towards a single aspect more, you'll either entertain people for a while (after which they forget about it) or there's a chance they find it boring. Videos give you a lot of creative freedom and depending on your business, we can recommend a number of different ideas including:

- A video tour of your physical store that shows off the different products and product categories you have for sale.
- Employee videos where you showcase your work culture and certain parts of your business that clients can resonate with. This is very useful if you're selling custom made items.
- Information of value that your core audience resonates with.
- Public service announcements or updates from the CEO.

- Testimonials that are a clear display of how your products/services directly benefit the prospects.
- Interviews with influential people in your area of expertise.
- Step-by-step guides showcasing how to use or set-up your product.
- Behind the scenes and/or day-in-the-life type of videos.

General Video Creation Process – How We Produce Engaging Sales Videos For Your
Business

We Start With The End Result In Mind

We understand that there is more to executing an effective video marketing strategy than simply making videos. We get to the bottom of what your target audience is really eager to find out, what their pain points are, the different angles we can cover, as well as your vision for how you want it to look.

Look For The Subtleties

We do thorough research and gather up as much information before we proceed with the video making process. All this research basically helps us create the type of video that people can actually engage with and respond to emotionally so that you immediately start drawing attention.

Often times we write a script (you can provide yours) if the video doesn't feature real life situations and then we take advantage of professional software to make it worth your prospect's time. The video we end up making is going to be a reflection on all the research we've conducted as well as your vision of what your ideal brand perception should be. It's a reflection of how you envision it looking ideally in a prospect's mind.

Sound

This is just as important because it goes hand in hand with a good video. We can basically add music or have a professional voiceover artist record for us before putting the finishing touches. We make sure that the voiceover artists we utilize know exactly what the tonality should be like, which value points to emphasize more than others, and make a variation of recordings so we end up using the ones that are most appropriate.

Approval Stage

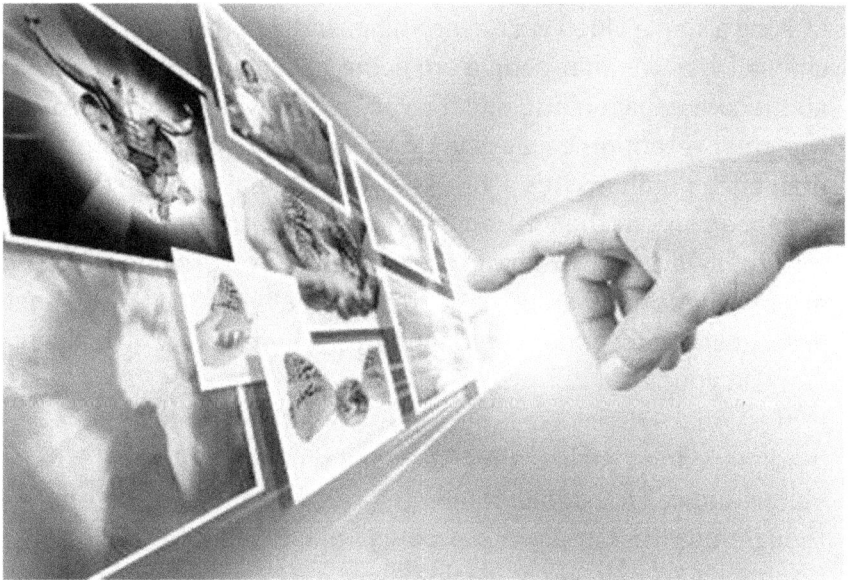

As soon as we've added those finishing touches, we'll get in touch with you (you'll be updated on progress) to see whether it fulfills your vision. We usually encourage people to connect with you either directly on the website or through other social media mediums. The point is to make that first impression and get them to engage more.

Mistakes That Kill An Effective Video Strategy

- There are plenty of mistakes people end up making that ultimately kill their brand vision and this is usually when attempting to make a video go viral. For instance, stuffing a video full of keywords doesn't necessarily mean that it's going to rank well nor will it attract the right kind of attention. There are certain rules you have to abide by and elements of randomness that are simply out of your control. The only thing we can actually control is the creative aspect and this is why we emphasize quality over quantity. If we do everything right (as mentioned in the process above) people will spread the video by themselves and do all the hard work for you.
- Making a single video isn't everything, and you have to structure a channel in a way that people are going to expect more. This is all about core engagement, and it's very useful when it comes to customer retention because you can use it with a number of marketing mediums. It's a lot easier to get email prospects hooked on video content than it is to make them purchase something straight away. Consistency in the value that you provide is key, and after we've conducted the research on what your target audience is likely going to respond to over and over, there is very little that can stand in your way.
- Professional videos take time. This is something that a lot of marketers don't realize; thus, they end up uploading mediocre videos and call it video marketing. A video needs to be carefully thought out the same way a product would, and it requires a lot of attention to detail by people who have experience as well as a great understanding of customer's psychology. If you're cooking a meal for others, they'll instinctively expect it to be warm, otherwise you'll face negative feedback. It's better to avoid uploading videos completely if you feel as if they're not up to par or ready for mass consumption. Video often times helps you make a first impression in a matter of seconds, which is not far off from graphic design.

What We Do To Ensure A Successful Video Marketing Strategy:

We Don't Make It An Afterthought

We understand that a lot of marketers are jumping on the video bandwagon merely because it's the hot thing at the moment, and they don't strategize enough before deploying their videos. A video has to be a reflection of your product's core values and it needs to convey that in a clear manner to people who have a partial/minimal interest in what you have to offer. Making sure we address the different pain points your customers are facing and providing a clear strategy to overcoming those is the only way we can ensure you get a head start to making your mark in a particular industry. It's about working smarter, not harder.

We Use Skilled Professionals

Outdated technology can kill a video promotion as well. You can have the best presentation out there, but if you record it with a low-quality camera or you don't have the right voiceovers, people will sense that carelessness right away. There are certain standards we make sure to go by (regardless of type of video) such as uploading only high quality HD formats, making sure the videos flow as they're supposed to and that the message gets across through a number of different "aha" moments.

We Draw Attention In A Favorable Way

The goal is to make that first impression a good one. The introduction part is what will either grab the viewer's attention or make them proceed with whatever it is they were doing beforehand. To ensure people are actually paying attention, we do so much research that they're instantly hooked after the first few seconds and have a general idea of what's to come. This is called the hook point and is one of those things that can add to your bottom line profits as it happens in a matter of seconds and the prospect doesn't realize it.

We Make Them Take Action

You're likely aware of the importance of call to action; hence, a natural consequence to not having one (even if you've kept them attentive throughout) means that they'll have nowhere to go after that. Depending on the type of business you're operating, and the different objectives our team helps you create from the start, you'll either aim to make them subscribe, share, or visit your website directly. There are different kinds of actions the average user can take, and choosing the right one at the end is crucial to your marketing strategy.

We Plant Seeds For The Future

We realize that video is merely a marketing channel for your business but it's an essential one at that. Choosing to utilize our video services means that you're ready to take control of your video marketing efforts and do it the right way because you realize you only have seconds to hook a potential customer. We'll show you the different ways to bridge an amazing video marketing strategy along with a number of other proven marketing strategies so you can maximize your earning potential and instantly boost user engagement.

Mobile Marketing

Mobile marketing is one of the best ways for you to enlarge the audience you're able to connect with and do so efficiently. You'll find there is a whole range of benefits for your business, even if you hadn't considered it in the past. We'd like to leave out the promises in terms of earning potential (this is obvious!) and focus directly on the facts and what you can actually do right now to get started.

Similar to the days when building a website for your business became absolutely mandatory as more and more customers started requesting it, you will now need a mobile-enabled presence to survive in a competing industry. The start of this year marked the first time in history when more than half of all Americans used their smartphones and tablets for Internet access ahead of desktop PCs. That number is rising fast, and globally.

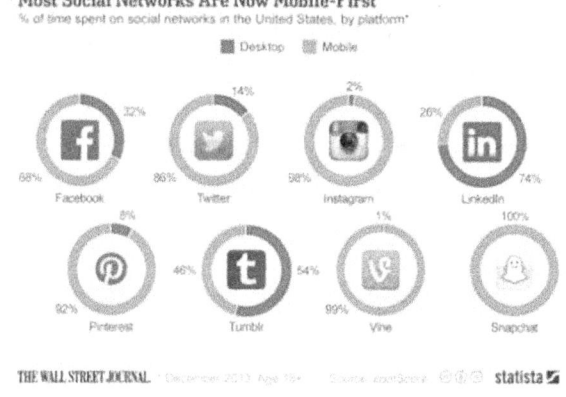

The new statistics in relation to mobile usage will blow your mind. For instance, a lot of countries in Africa skipped straight to the mobile revolution, and even though their populations didn't have desktops at large, they now do so with smartphones. More than 50% of all adults in the US own a smartphone, and that figure goes up to nearly 80% when you consider the smartphone usage in the worldwide population. The interesting fact to mention here is that only a very low percentage of websites out there are properly optimized for mobile access; consequently, utilizing our services will put you ahead of the curve. You'll probably be interested in learning about mobile advertising and the impact social network traffic has on the smartphone industry. Also, what are the essential differences between smartphone/tablet users and desktop users? We're going to address that right now.

Personalization

There are very few benefits out there that work in your favor as much as personalization does because mobile phones are personal in nature. People carry them around all the time and most check them every few minutes, even when they're on silent mode. Think of it this way: Let's say you choose to put up the biggest billboard in a busy area of your city. Even though you know a lot of people are ultimately going to walk/drive by and see it, you're not actually giving them personal attention the way you would with mobile marketing. Adding a personal touch is more than necessary for brand recognition and loyalty. Around 50% of all email is also opened on a mobile device; hence, optimization is also useful for your email marketing.

Immediate Global Reach

There has never been a time in history where we had access to the same immediate options that mobile access currently offers us. We can reach anyone, anywhere, and at any time. Making it easy for people to obtain information about your product in only a few seconds is going to increase your business potential by a huge margin, and this is only projected to grow in the future.

Penetration Rates Are Higher

Considering that there are tens of billions of smartphones out there, realize that there are a lot more people visiting the Internet through a mobile device than there are on a desktop. If you're working in a fairly unknown industry, you might even reach an untapped audience.

Specific SMS Advertising

This is yet another tool for your arsenal, and if you make it a part of your lead generation strategy, you can immediately reach people who you want to see certain campaigns of yours.

Take in consideration the fact that there are thousands of products which keep coming out on a daily basis and very few that actually stand out. What the different types of mobile marketing have in common is they let your target audience know exactly who you are, what you're offering, and the type of products you have before allowing them to take action on it.

This is becoming the most popular way of marketing, and you can only look forward to the future developments as your business grows by getting started right now. There are also a lot of creative options, which are untapped, and you have the advantage of situational impulse. For instance, if someone is out shopping, they take a break to check their phone and stumble upon your offer--the odds are extremely high that they'll end up purchasing your product or saving it for later.

62

Great In Combination With Other Marketing Channels

We encourage our clients to focus on providing value to a core audience over the long term and an audience, which keeps growing until they've taken up a significant portion of an industry. It's in your best interest to look for ways to increase your customer retention and loyalty; hence, this is one of the most effective ways to build that desirable list.

Tracking Options

Similar to regular email marketing, you can track the overall message delivery and response rate easily.

Things That Make Or Break A Mobile Marketing Strategy: Misusage Of SEO Techniques

SEO quickly became popular a few years ago when people were hiring agencies to help them build up a network of sites and rank them for certain keywords up until Google made the Penguin and Panda updates. Ever since then, the techniques in ranking have changed a lot and if you paid for some SEO work before 2012, you might want to revise those techniques as they could work against you.

Here's what you should keep in mind: Search engines are now more aware than ever whether you're using outdated tricks or not. They have a zero tolerance policy for technical errors, and if you've had your website optimized even as early as a few years ago, you should check everything again with us to make sure it's on point.

You'll need a website that is both optimized for mobile access, search engines, and one that is properly coded. This is to make sure the positions you retain don't eventually go down as the result of an algorithm update.

How Do We Address This?

We basically update/optimize every single page of your website, your presence on social media, new email campaigns, separate mobile pages, and campaigns which work with today's standards and provide information that the search engines are looking for to properly index all your assets. We also make sure to bring forward how fresh your content really is, make it sharable, and use a number of different strategies to keep you on top over the long term. We're not focused on short-term results.

Lack Of Interesting, Quality Content

Often times people will tell you the importance of content in regular text form or the importance of video, but one thing that can really affect your rankings in a bad way is if you're using old content which hasn't been updated. If the majority of your pages only have a few paragraphs worth of text, or the content hasn't been updated in years, you'll likely stay on top if you don't have blood-hungry competitors, but search engines won't hesitate to drop you in favor of fresh information.

How Do We Solve This?

We review your entire website for quality of content, make sure it's sharable, and show you ways to fix everything in a way that both search engines, as well as readers on different platforms, will find it pleasing. We also develop maintenance strategies that will ensure new content gets added to your website that promotes further customer engagement (in combination to other marketing mediums).

Lack Of Device Optimization

- There are billions of smartphones in the world today. Most Americans under the age of 18 have multiple devices.
- Studies indicate that well over 60% of mobile users say that if the website doesn't load properly within the first 3 seconds, they likely won't search for it ever again.
- Statistic shows that about half of all mobile users said that even if they were fans of a certain brand, they would use it a lot less on their mobile device if it didn't load right the first time.

The main thing you should know about mobile websites is that they're not the same as desktop--they have a lot less content and are about as focused as they can get. You'll find the majority of mobile websites include features such as call to action social media, thumb friendly navigation, etc. You're probably familiar with how hard it is to open up an entire desktop website on a small mobile device and have to pinch your way around to get the necessary information.

What We Focus On To Deliver An Effective Mobile Marketing Strategy: Making Things Simple

We try to simplify your mobile presence to emphasize the main key points of value and quickly cut off things that are unnecessary. Simplicity is key in making an effective mobile marketing strategy, and if your site is heavy on content by nature, it's going to be very hard for them to navigate their way around. We stick to minimalistic websites and promotional campaigns that get the point across and let people get immediate access to the information they're in need of.

Ensuring Efficiency

We make sure to support all leading mobile and tablet devices. We don't just optimize your website for optimal functioning in different browsers but mobile devices as well. There isn't a single standard that works across all the different mobile devices, but addressing the issue in the first place (for at least the most popular devices) is what will keep a lot of them coming back.

Making Them Snappy

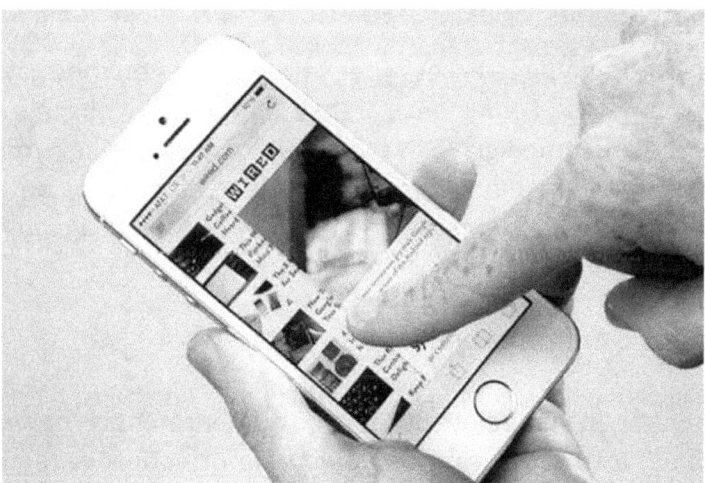

A major epiphany that came through research and testing was that not all of our customers had the fastest connection or used the latest of gadgets. Even though a webpage can open up flawlessly on an expensive smartphone with a decent Internet connection, this isn't always the case on cheaper devices. We focus on providing a good experience for both people who are using cutting edge technology as well as ones that don't have the latest of gadgets.

Creating A Separate Marketing Campaign

Even with the simplest of things, such as SEO keyword targeting, we're well aware of the differences in behavior patterns. For instance, if a person is using a desktop computer, and they have a specific problem to solve, they'll likely type in longer keywords. However, if they're on the go and need answers fast the majority will only type a keyword or two at most. Small adjustments like optimizing for that can make a world of difference.

Ensuring Recognition And Redirection

Before a visitor is able to access your smartphone site, they have to be redirected to it first. For instance, if they land on the website from an email marketing campaign you've sent out, or a simple keyword search, the systems we put in place are able to identify the device they're using and then send them to a separate page designed for that device.

Cutting Out Unnecessary Requirements

We found that an immediate boost in customer retention on smartphones is to decrease the amount of information we require from them and focus on providing value instead. Filling in information is not that desirable with desktops and even more so on a smartphone. If you have to make them fill out a form, we usually recommend you keep it as simple as the email and password.

Maximizing Action

As mentioned earlier, you have that situational impulse working in your favor when dealing with mobile traffic as people can be anywhere and still get to your message in a matter of minutes. We devise plans to clearly address where the different call to actions should be: when to make them share, email, like or directly purchase. This ultimately gives you more freedom to work on improving your product and sets you up for success in the long term.

Reputation Management (add-on service)

Information about every company out there is available at the fingertips of all and even the big companies are having a hard time with reputation management. Word of mouth marketing is taking on a whole new meaning with social media and the fact that people are globally and instantaneously connected; therefore, reputation management has become essential.

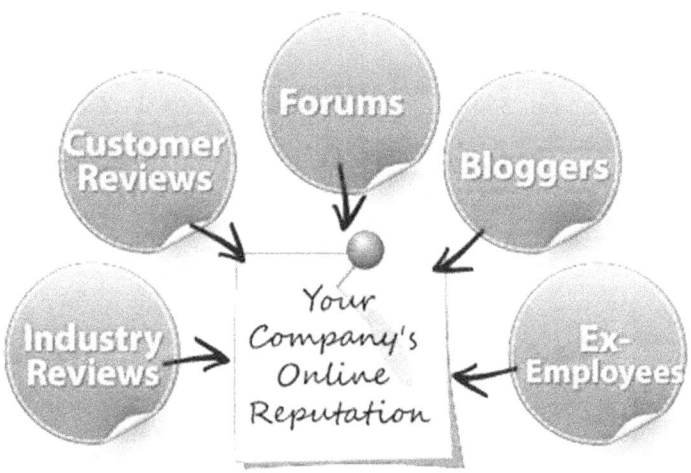

People are not afraid to voice their opinion (especially a negative one), and there are outlets that encourage them to do so, and thus it's becoming harder for a subpar quality brand to make its way to the top. The minute you put a business out there, it's going to draw attention, and this could amount to amazing things or just as well turn into a never ending nightmare. Which side do you want to be on?

For our marketing efforts, we utilize the most advanced of technology and work with people from different marketing backgrounds to come up with a unique strategy for each business. Even then, we place high importance on the customer feedback as well as the preservation of our client's reputation. A study recently indicated that nearly 70% of people ended up making a decision based on either social media presence or feedback shared by past customers online. As soon as your business starts gaining traction, the key to preserving it and expanding long-term is to proceed offering value but simultaneously making sure more people are on your good side than on the bad. There is no way to get around that.

Reputation management is an entire industry whose sole focus is on managing the overall perception of a particular brand or person, then promoting content that works in its favor. Often times desperate competitors will go as far as spreading negative information about a product/service for the sole intention of diverting traffic to their offer. There are lots of variables that take place, and this is especially true for brands that are seeing massive growth spikes unexpectedly.

Who Can Benefit From Reputation Management?

Every company with an interest in preserving a generally positive outlook for their brand as well as popular individuals (entertainers, athletes, artists, etc.) can benefit from reputation management. You have to realize that negative feedback is inevitable, regardless of the quality of product you're putting out, and that's why it's better to be prepared from the start.

When it comes to online reputation management services, this is actually one of the fastest growing industries out there and proof enough of that is the fact that when the EU allowed citizens to request the removal of their information from Google, nearly a hundred thousand requests were sent out in the first week.

Reasons Why Reputation Management Is Useful

There are different variables to understand, but considering the growing demand for this service, here are the main ones:

- Reputation matters for all business owners because a negative reputation impacts your business. It matters for everyone, from the small town gossip and embarrassment that comes from negative reviews and customer complaints that affects the small mom pop businesses all the way up to the large corporations. You can see real life examples everywhere: BP and the Gulf of Mexico spill. Malaysia Airlines and the plane that was lost in the Southern Indian Ocean. There is very little that can be done to reverse a situation like that. However, in a less severe case it's certainly manageable. What you should realize is that your business might be missing out on a lot of prospective clients if the first ranked websites are mostly negative reviews.

- We're all connected and can find out anything in a matter of seconds. If someone is considering purchasing your product and their friends haven't tried it yet, they can easily look into reviews (or social media sites) to see whether you're the real deal. People look for reinforcement now more than ever, and decisions are made in a matter of minutes. There are also forums, rip-off review sites, customer reviews, blogs, etc., all encouraging or diverting people away from your business.

- Even if the general perception of your brand is that it provides value, the fact still remains that every bit of information, which is out there and indexed by the search engines, is next to impossible to erase.

How Do You Protect Your Reputation?

You can start by monitoring the things that are being said, as there are a number of tools to help you achieve that. One of the best tools is Google Alerts, although you'll only be notified of it, and there are still not that many options if negative reviews are brought to the forefront.

If you do notice a lot of negative reviews/comments that have been made by customers, or even some of your competitors, there are effective ways to repair the situation. We offer some of the best reputation management services for brands, but we'll still let you know what some of the obvious things not to do are.

Things You Shouldn't Do

We've noticed instances in which business owners have made a situation worse by responding to it when they could have easily dealt with it quietly:

- Not paying attention to what your customers are saying can be detrimental. This is about the biggest mistake you can make and should be the first thing you do instinctively if you're trying to make it through a tough situation. You need to have a thorough understanding of everything your customers go through so that you have complete understanding of how to fulfill your customer's needs.

- Treating your customers in an unfriendly or disrespectful fashion is a recipe for disaster. This is an obvious one, though it's not uncommon for business owners to treat their customers in a disrespectful manner. You have to know how to hold your own even when you're dealing with harsh feedback, and realize that you'll likely learn more from that than you would from good feedback. In the best possible scenario, you should put all your efforts in resolving a dispute rather than focusing in on personal attacks.

Our General Aims

We're very experienced in managing reputation, but we also realize that it's extremely hard to remove negative information, which has accumulated for a business, except in instances where it's downright offensive/slanderous, and we can prove that the information is false.

We mainly focus on the suppression side of things that will allow you to coast by and expand just fine, although if you have a number of unsatisfied customers who like to voice their opinion and even hate your business with a passion--that can be irreversible. The key here is to make the changes necessary so that when a new prospect looks up information on your product, they end up seeing results that are favorable. Here are some of the things we can do for you:

Help You Take Charge Of The Situation

The important thing is that you take control of the dispute that is currently in place by using a number of resources. In the past, if a company wanted to rebuild its reputation they would normally have to pay for expensive television ads that in turn made them look good although there are much more effective mediums now.

For instance, our social media specialist can easily improve the outlook of your company by describing what improvements you've made, how you went about resolving current issues, and emphasizing the improvements you'll make in the future. The goal is to not only improve your current reputation but rather put you in a position where the scenario couldn't possibly develop again, thus leaving you with room for improvement/growth.

Quickly Neutralize Threats

Threats to your reputation can come from a range of sources, and the good thing is that we're using some of the most sophisticated tools to help us monitor everything that is in important relation to your brand so that when we do notice threats coming up, we can easily get them out of the way. As we mentioned earlier, negative feedback finds its way to the surface even when you're consistent in providing value; hence, an approach where you actually learn to expect it is ideal because it couldn't hit you by surprise.

Handling It Discretely

We're experienced marketing experts, and we know exactly the struggles that an upcoming company can go through, especially in a competitive industry where people will take every measure to get ahead. If you're trying to save on time and money that will help you further improve your product, it's best that you let us completely take over the reputation management side of things, and we can also help you repair and re-build your current reputation to a favorable one. We have everything from experienced content writers to seasoned social media managers, and we know how to discretely go about achieving desirable results for your company.

To Conclude

I really hope that you enjoyed this guide and found the concepts inside it useful. If you did, we encourage you to share it with a colleague who you think is going to find it beneficial as well.

These concepts and principles listed here have proven effective over and over again in a number of different industries, thus, you should consider implementing some (or all) as soon as possible. There are certainly other avenues you can explore marketing wise, and this whitepaper isn't the be-all and end-all; however, these are strategies that can be considered the platform to a successful marketing campaign and will eventually require implementation if you plan to see growth.

In order for you to make everything work, you'll have to invest at least a few thousand dollars initially and have a quality product/service already in place. In case you don't have a website, we recommend you let our team take over the development process as we're going to create one in alignment to a unique marketing approach.

Get in touch with us if you'd like to learn more about pricing and schedule a free consultation to see if we can work together to help elevate or initiate your marketing strategy the right way.

To receive content on how video marketing can help your business generate more leads, sales and revenue click the links below.

Learn how video marketing can help you business

Custom Video Commercials How It Benefits You

Powerful Statistics On Video Marketing For Small Businesses

Lets Summarize How Video Marketing Can Benefit Your Business

If you enjoy my work, please feel free to join my mailing list at:

http://www.videoseowarrior.com/videomarketing

You can also follow me on Facebook at:

http://www.facebook.com/pages/Darkam-Marketing-Services

You can also follow me on LinkedIn at:

https://www.linkedin.com/in/richardrobertsmarketing

And if you are interested in learning more about my other products and publications, please visit:

http://www.richardrobertsmarketing.com

Best wishes in your endeavors!

Richard Roberts

www.ingramcontent.com/pod-product-compliance
Lightning Source LLC
Chambersburg PA
CBHW070844180526
45168CB00002B/954